GERMANY

A PICTURE MEMORY

Text
Bill Harris

Captions
Pauline Graham

Design
Teddy Hartshorn

Photography
Colour Library Books Ltd
Tim Sharman

Editorial
Jane Adams
Pauline Graham

Production
Ruth Arthur
Sally Connolly
David Proffit
Andrew Whitelaw

Director of Production
Gerald Hughes

Commissioning
Andrew Preston
Edward Doling
Laura Potts

CLB 2521

This 1993 edition published by Magna Books,
Magna Road, Wigston, Leicester LE18 4ZH
Printed and bound in Singapore
ISBN 1-85422-530-8

GERMANY

A PICTURE MEMORY

MAGNA BOOKS

6.25

First page: Schloss Neuschwanstein perched over Pöllat Gorge in the Bavarian Alps. This castle was built by "Mad King Ludwig," or Ludwig II. Münden (previous pages), Lower Saxony, was founded in about 1170 by Henry the Lion on the spot where, according to an old German rhyme, the rivers "Werra and Fulda kiss each other and lose their own names to become the river Weser." Facing page: Heidelberg's Alte Brücke (Old Bridge) over the River Neckar.

On Christmas Day, 1989, a lot of people found something under their tree that would have been completely unthinkable the year before. It was a highly significant symbol of new hope for the 'nineties: a piece of the Berlin Wall. The Wall had seemed like it was going to be a permanent fixture for so long that most of us who cheered when it came down could hardly remember why it went up in the first place.

It was, in fact, the brainchild of the Communist boss of East Germany, Walter Ulbricht, who said he had built the twenty-eight-mile-long barrier to protect his people from "fascists" on the other side. They were kidnapping the brightest and best of his people, he said, and filling the heads of workers and farmers with radical ideas. On the western side it was regarded as a spite fence, and became a target for political oratory and graffiti.

Ulbricht had been the butt of many jokes ever since his young days as a budding Marxist when his grade-school companions nicknamed him "Red." Even his most ardent followers considered him a bumbler. But if Comrade Ulbricht was often portrayed as a fool, it was far from a true picture of him, and while the Berlin Wall was not exactly a stroke of genius, it was not the spiteful act of a megalomaniac either.

When Germany was divided after the end of World War II, thousands in the Russian-dominated East began heading across the border into the newly-created Federal Republic. Many were anti-Communist, others were frustrated by the bureaucracy of the East and some simply wanted to be with their families in the West. More than a quarter of them were young people lured Westward by better educational opportunities. During the first seven years of the occupation, when crossing the border was as simple as walking through the forest, nearly 800,000 people made the trip. In the early 1950s, security was tightened and refugees began taking vacations in West Germany and then defecting while there. By the time travel restrictions were formulated, about a million more East Germans had taken the trip. The restrictions were severe and succeeded in stemming the tide, but there was still one avenue of escape open to them. Berlin, though located within East Germany, was divided into sectors controlled by the various occupying nations. Anyone in the Russian sector could board a subway into the American zone and from there catch a plane to the West without even bothering to look back. By 1961, an estimated twenty percent of East Germany's population had moved across the border, and the result was nothing short of chaos. Stores were shuttered because their owners had moved on, schools closed because there were no teachers, factories lost their skilled workers, fields went untended because farmers had fled. Villages were without medical care when doctors moved away and cities faced coming to a standstill through a lack of plumbers, electricians and even bus drivers. From Ulbricht's point of view, a wall across Berlin was the only answer.

It stood there for twenty-eight years, an ugly symbol for most and a challenge for many. Though hundreds were killed trying to cross it, hundreds more succeeded, often with ingenious schemes that would put spy novels to shame. They used tightropes and miniature submarines, tunnels and elaborate disguises, but most East Germans resigned themselves to the inevitable and decided to make the best of a bad thing. In less than a decade, they had the highest standard of living in the Communist world and their state was well on the way to taking its place among the world's great industrial powers.

Now, after forty-five years of isolation from the West, the German Democratic Republic has pulled back the curtain and the land that gave the world Johann Sebastian Bach and Martin Luther is open once again for a business almost as alien to the Communist world as Wall Street itself, the tourist business. What the visitors are seeing is a restoration of some of the magnificence of Dresden and the Old-World charm of Rostock. Many of these places are drab and somber by Western standards, but the traditional home of the Saxons and Prussians has taken on a new lease of life that, during the 1960s, seemed as impossible as the prospect of finding a piece of the Berlin Wall for sale in a New York department store.

These days the debate over whether the two Germanies should be united again has driven people as far apart as discussions on the relative merits of Communism versus Capitalism. But the fact is that at the end of World War II, the German nation that was split in two was less than seventy-five years old.

It was created in 1871 when William I, the Hohenzollern King of Prussia, took control of no less than twenty-five separate kingdoms. The people were given the right to elect their own National Assembly, but the legislature's lower house, the *Reichstag*, where elected deputies served, had no direct power over the government except for matters of funding. The upper house, the *Bundesrat*, was filled with appointed nobles, and both were controlled by the Chancellor, who answered to no one but the Emperor himself, and the Emperor knew better than to challenge the Chancellor, one Otto Von Bismarck.

Bismarck was one of the most significant German figures of the nineteenth century. He had reorganized the Prussian army that defeated the Austrians in 1866 and negotiated a peace treaty that cleared the way to unite Germany. He had also cultivated control of the Prussian bureaucracy. His skilled foreign diplomacy put Germany firmly onto the world stage, and he led his country to the forefront of the world's great industrial powers. But as industry developed, the "Iron Chancellor" began to face problems even he could not handle. Socialists were flexing their muscles in the factories and, though Bismarck tried buying them off with such things as the world's first health insurance program and retirement benefits, what they really wanted was power in the *Reichstag*. As more and more of them were elected, the Chancellor became more and more frustrated, finally suggesting to the Emperor that the only way to put the Socialists in their place was to abolish the Constitution. The Kaiser responded by firing him. Much to Bismarck's surprise, Germany survived without him.

Germany had survived many worse blows over the centuries. The first ruler they knew was Clovis, the Emperor of the Franks, who crossed the Rhine in 486 bent on converting the Arians to Christianity, making slaves of them at the same time. His descendants ruled for three centuries before power passed through their fingers – ironically because their subjects had become Christianized and welcomed missionaries from England and Ireland into their midst. Chief among them was Boniface, who organized the Catholic Church there and made an official named Pepin King of the Germans. Pepin's son, Charles, who is remembered by his Frankish name, Charlemagne, continued the work, and succeeded in conquering all of central Europe. It was the first time since the fall of Rome that so much territory was brought under the control of a single ruler. In the year 800, the Pope officially recognized the accomplishment by making Charlemagne Emperor of the Holy Roman Empire.

His fifty-year-long reign was more German than Roman, however, and centered power on himself rather than on laws that would have survived him. When he died, the government of his empire crumbled at the hands of a collection of feuding nobility. He had started the ball rolling himself when he decreed that the empire should be divided among his three sons. The problem of who would get what was solved when two of his sons died before he did. The survivor, Louis the Pious, decided that his own three sons would be heirs to the kingdom, but there was a problem: Louis had four sons. His second wife, mother of the unanticipated Charles, began a campaign of intrigue to make sure her son got what she thought was coming to him. By the time Louis died, the brothers were all at each other's throats and hardly noticed that there was a kingdom waiting to be divided. It took them two years to settle their differences, during which time ambitious princes had grabbed almost all the power.

By the time they stopped fighting among themselves, one of the four brothers was dead, two had divided the territory east and west of the Rhine between them and the third, Lothar, was given the Rhine Valley between the North Sea and Italy as a sort of consolation prize. In the centuries since, the map of Europe has changed dozens of times, but the boundaries of France and Germany as well as the politics of the two countries dates back to the treaty that settled the squabbling among these brothers.

Charlemagne's legacy was a close tie to the papacy. Over the next few centuries, the German king was the temporal head of all of Christendom. He had the power to appoint or remove a pope as well bishops and abbots. The Church provided him with an efficient bureaucracy and a mediator to help him handle the differences among the tribes under his control.

The arrangement began to fall apart when King Henry III died in 1056. His son and heir was only six years old, so the job of running the empire fell on the shoulders of the boy king's mother. Pope Leo IX, who was the boy's second cousin, took advantage of the situation by convening a council that decreed future popes would be elected by the College of Cardinals. A few years later, Pope Gregory VII went a step further by declaring that no king had the right to appoint bishops either. Since Henry IV was the only King who had that power, Henry responded by saying that Gregory's election had been invalid and that he was going to go right on appointing bishops. Gregory countered by excommunicating the King.

The German nobles saw this to be a signal that the time was ripe to grab some power for themselves. In the midst of the war that followed, Henry IV was overthrown by his own son and tossed into a dungeon, but not before he made Clement III Pope and banished Gregory into exile. Henry V spent the rest of his life fighting with Rome over who had the power to appoint bishops. The issue was settled in a compromise that limited the king's control over the German clergy and eliminated his influence in the rest of the world.

The real losers in the long fight were the German people. While emperors and popes were locking horns, neither had time to keep an eye on the self-serving nobility. By the time their squabbling was over, the nobles had all the real power and the people were forced to become allied with them for protection.

During the Middle Ages more than 2,000 new towns and cities sprang up all over the German landscape. People felt safer behind their high stone walls and enjoyed special privileges, not the least of which was protection from the private wars the aristocracy were continually waging among themselves. Almost all of the cities, both new and old, became overcrowded but there were many compensations.

Every town had at least one broad avenue that led to the town square where foreigners often gathered to sell their wares along with the produce of the local market. The buildings around the square were designed to impress visitors, as they still do, and give the residents of the city a better self-image. A magnificent cathedral was usually built in these cities, near the town hall, known as the *Rathaus*, and another building, just as impressive, called the *Kaufhaus*, a base for the local merchants. The *Rathaus* was the most important building in town. It was where the council deliberated and where banqueting and dancing was staged on feast days. It was where magistrates meted out justice and its basement held the city jail. But the basement had an even better use. It was the *Ratskeller*, where the city's supply of beer and wine were stored under the watchful eye of the *Bürgermeister*.

The wars that raged outside the city walls affected everyone. The Church itself finally stepped in, threatening nobles with excommunication if their armies touched the property of either the Church or private citizens. Later, the rule was expanded into what was known as the "truce of God," prohibiting warfare from Wednesday through Monday and during all of Lent. The truce was followed faithfully for more than a century until the Pope had a better idea. Instead of fighting brother against brother and destroying local farms, he said, why not go to the Holy Land and free Jerusalem from the Infidel?

The first of the Crusades, called for by Pope Urban II in 1095, was almost completely a French affair. The Germans picked up the cause in 1147 when the second wave headed for the Holy Sepulcher, but went down in defeat. The Third Crusade, which actually reached Jerusalem, was begun by the German Emperor Frederick Barbarossa in 1189. He was an impressive, red-bearded man with 20,000 enthusiastic knights in his train. Even more impressive was the fact that he was seventy years old when the Crusade began.

Frederick was considered by his people to be the greatest emperor Germany ever had. His goal was to restore the empire to its original glory, and he very nearly succeeded. He was able to put an end to private wars and managed to bring new territory under German influence. However, it transpired that his reign marked the last gasp of his great German Empire. He never came back from his crusade, nor did his son. By the time the Pope called for another march on the Holy Land, war was raging at home over succession to the throne, so the Germans sat that one out. Then, in 1212, someone had the brilliant idea that if Jerusalem was ever to be returned to Christian hands, the hands must belong to the purest and most innocent of all Christians, little children. Thousands of German youngsters marched away but almost none got any further than the Italian port of Genoa where they died or were sold into slavery. This incident cooled German ardor for crusading. Of the three marches that followed, German knights marched in only one.

A holy crusade of quite another type began in at the University of Wittenberg in Saxony on Halloween night in 1517 when a professor of Bible Studies nailed a list of "Ninety-five Theses" to the door of a church. Among them was the revolutionary idea that selling salvation to the highest bidder, the practice of selling indulgences, was sinful in itself. Within weeks of the poster's appearance, the whole Christian world was aware of the ideas of the Augustinian monk, and his name, Martin Luther, was known to everyone. What made that possible was a German invention that changed the way the world thinks. Johann Gutenberg of Mainz had developed moveable metal type that made it possible to print

Facing page: a narrow street in Flensburg, Schleswig-Holstein, the northernmost port in Germany and gateway to Scandinavia. The town is famous for its blend of West Indian rum.

books and, by the time Martin Luther nailed his ideas to the church door, there were more than 1,000 printing presses in operation and some 30,000 separate books had already been printed. Luther was probably the first best-selling author.

The Protestant Reformation spread out from Germany into the world beyond. But the world was not quite ready to embrace its new ideas without a fight and the war that followed was fought on German soil, even though it was not a German war. It began in Bohemia as a rebellion against the Hapsburgs, who brought in troops from other countries to stop it and, in the process, to check the spread of Protestantism. That encouraged Protestant countries to send in troops of their own. The fighting did not stop for thirty years. In the end, the Germans found themselves under the control of Sweden and France, but the war had wiped out a quarter of the German population, and no city or town had escaped at least partial destruction. More than 30,000 villages had vanished forever, including the city of Magdeburg, which lost 25,000 of its citizens in less than an hour before Swedish troops burned it to the ground.

Life went on, of course, even though the old kingdom had broken up into some 300 little kingdoms, each with its own government, its own army and its own way of life. Saxony – its capital at Dresden – and Bavaria, whose center was the thriving city of Munich, both led the way to recovering lost German pride. But the most impressive of them all was the northen state of Brandenburg-Prussia, whose emperors, members of the Hohenzollern family, turned a ruined territory of about three quarters of a million into a kingdom of five million secured by one of the most powerful armies in the world. The stage was set for the creation of the modern Germany that was united again on October 3rd, 1990.

Of course, Germany as a unified nation of that name did not exist until after the American Civil War. It was built on a foundation of endless creation and re-creation of states by different Germanic tribes, dating from as far back as AD 9, when an exasperated Augustus declared the Rhine and the Danube to be the frontiers of the Roman Empire. It was unified as late as 1871 under the leadership of the Prussian prime minister Otto von Bismarck.

When all the politics are put aside and all the bloodshed forgotten, the land itself is filled with a special kind of charm that never fails to create an impression. Every era is very much alive there, from Roman ruins and medieval castles to modern cities. But most impressive are the people themselves. They constitute a Germany that is a special spirit in the heart of Europe. Now that the wall has come down between East and West, the whole world is watching to see what is likely to happen next. Germany's first attempts at unification began 1,500 years ago. Together again, and benefitting from the hard lessons of their history and two World Wars, there seems to be almost nothing Germany cannot accomplish.

Johannsen
CAP-
RUM
C.A.Petersen
FLENSBURG

CONCORDIA DOMI FORIS PAX

Flensburg (facing page top) grew into an elegant town by the Flensburger Förde, on the Danish border, by virtue of its naval base and trade in rum. Right: the Rathaus, Lübeck, and (facing page bottom) Lübeck's famous Holstentor, a massive gate built in 1477 in the town's famous Backsteingotik (brick Gothic) style. Below: Hostenstrasse, Kiel's main shopping precinct. Kiel, founded in 1233, is the capital of Schleswig-Holstein, and since the formation of the Deutsches Reich in 1871 has been the site of Germany's largest naval base.

These pages and overleaf: Hamburg. Above: a leafy path by the Binnenalster, overlooked by the Alsterpavillon Café (below left). Left: the Atlantic Hotel on the Aussenalster. From a waterside café (facing page) on the Alsterfleet (below) one can see the towered Rathaus (above left). Overleaf: Wedel on the Elbe, one of Hamburg's suburbs.

Facing page: the Rathaus on Fernhandelsmarkt, Lüneburg (these pages), Lower Saxony. Some of the gabled houses around this square, informally known as "Am Sande" ("on the sand") have subsided. Perhaps it stands on salt, for Lüneburg was built literally and economically on "white gold" atop a salt deposit, and its fortune was made by working and trading salt.

Tchibo
Bäckerei

These pages and overleaf: Berlin, capital of pre-World War II Germany, once more undivided. Above: the Soviet War Memorial. Above right: the Bismarck Memorial in the Tiergarten. Zitadelle Spandau (right), one of Europe's finest Renaissance water fortresses, housed Rudolf Hess until his death in 1987. From 1966, he was the prison's sole inmate. Facing page and below right: Schloss Charlottenburg. Below: the Neptune Fountain, Alexanderplatz. Overleaf: "the hollow tooth," war-ruined Kaiser Wilhelm Memorial Church.

JVC
HI-FI
VIDEO
JVC
COMPUR
MUNCHNER HOFBR
AEROFLOT
Soviet airlines
MUNCHNER
P

Schultheiss
U
Ende

Eisenach (above right), birthplace, in 1685, of J.S. Bach, was part of East Germany (these pages and overleaf) before unification on October 3, 1990. In Wartburg Castle (below), Martin Luther began his translation of the Bible*. Facing page and above: the hunting lodge of the Saxon Electors in Moritzburg, near Dresden. Quedlinburg (below right), founded in 922, was the birthplace of geographer Carl Ritter and poet Friedrich Gottlieb Klopstock. Overleaf: the Elbe where it forms the border with Czechoslovakia, seen from Bastei rock south of Dresden in the Erzegebirge Mountains.*

The statue of Charlemagne's Knight Roland (facing page), Bremen's symbol of freedom and independence, stands before the Renaissance façade of the fifteenth-century Rathaus (left) in the town's Marktplatz (these pages). Bremen is a historic city and Germany's oldest maritime town. It is said that the Saxons set off from here in 449 to conquer England. In 789, Charlemagne endowed Bremen with a bishopric, and from here Scandanavia was christianized.

MEHR VOM MEER

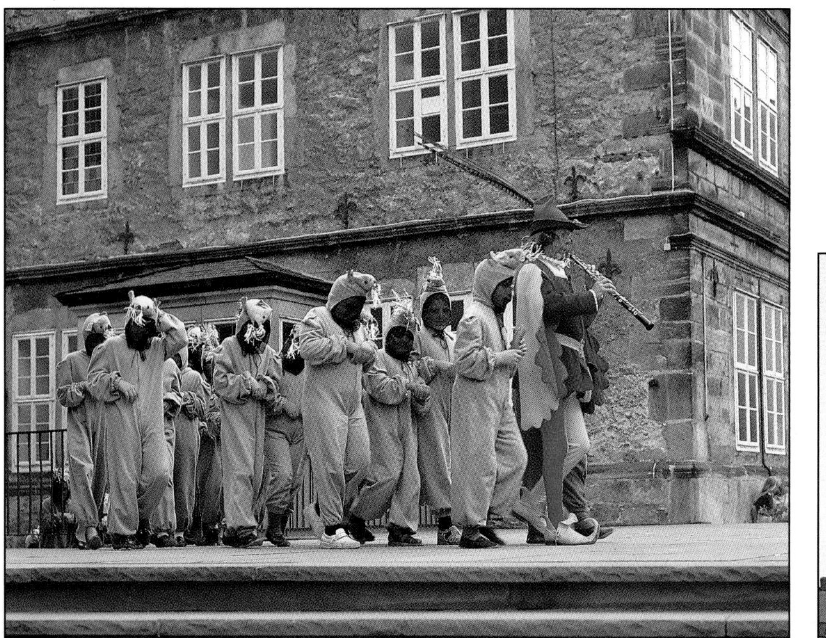

On the terrace (below) between the Hochzeitshaus, or wedding house, and the church of St. Nikolai in Hameln (these pages), citizens gather every Sunday during the summer months to reenact the Pied Piper story that has made the town famous all over the world. Some historians believe that Bundting, the piper, was a real person who was a land agent and took the 130 children to settle Pomerania and Sudetenland. Bottom left: Allemarkstrasse, and (below left) the Markt.

Hannover (these pages), the capital of Lower Saxony, gives the impression of modern bustle and industry. Much of the city is indeed modern, rebuilt after substantial damage was inflicted on it during World War II. Over sixty percent of the old town was destroyed. Nonetheless, historical buildings still stand, linking modern Hannover with its illustrious past. Unfortunately, one of the buildings lost was the home of Gottfried Wilhelm Leibniz (1646-1716), the famous philosopher who laid the foundations of integral and differential calculus and formulated the binary system of numeration. Facing page: the railway station. Hannover is one of Germany's most important traffic junctions.

DB
Zum 150 Geburtstag:
Restaurant

DB
HH
HANNOVER HÄNDEL
HERRENHAUSEN
Ein Fest mit Georg Friedrich Händel
Hannover, Großer Garten Herrenhausen 21., 22., 23., 28., 29., 30., Juni - 5., 6., 7., Juli 1985

Facing page: (top) Schloss Senden, near Wasserburg, and (bottom) Burg Vischering, Lüdinghausen. Above: Koblenz Gate, Bonn, once part of the Electors' Residence (below right), now the Friedrich-Wilhelms-Universität. Right: Poppelsdorf Schloss, Bonn. Above right: Dom St. Paul, Münster. Below: Münster's Lambertikirche. The three cages in its latticed tower were used to exhibit the bodies of Anabaptist leaders after their movement was crushed in 1536. Overleaf: Köln (Cologne).

IBM

Zur Badstube
Weinstuben

Weinhaus Klein
Markthalle

Left: the angular, beam-bisected houses of Karlstrasse in Bernkastel-Kues, a town which encompasses two towns straddling the Mosel River. Below left: the seventeenth-century Michaelsbrunnen fountain in Bernkastel's sloping Markt. Below: Monschau on the Rur, a small Eifel town near the Belgian border, blends scenically with the countryside around the High Venn.

Above: the Marktplatz, Michelstadt. Burg Klopp stands sentry over the old town of Bingen (above left) on the confluence of the Nahe and the Rhein. Left and below left: the seven-spired Dom, or Collegiate and Parish Church of St. Georg and St. Nikolaus, on the Lahn at Limburg. Below: Schloss Mespelbrunn in the Spessart Mountains of Bavaria. Facing page: (top) Münden, and (bottom) Hirschhorn on the Neckar. Overleaf: the Main river, from Frankfurt's Flösserbrücke.

Above: Kamp-Bornhofen, a Franciscan pilgrimage center on the Rhein (these pages). Above left: the Mäuseturm at Bingen. Left: Marksburg. Below left: the Benedictine convent of St. Hildegard, Eibingen, near Rüdesheim. Below: Drosselgasse in Rüdesheim. Facing page: (top) Assmannshausen, once a wine village famous for its red wine, now part of Rüdesheim, and (bottom) the island fortress of Pfalzgrafenstein in the Rhein, which was built as a customs house. Overleaf: Burg Reichenstein above Trechtingshausen.

Facing page top and overleaf: lofty Reichsburg Cochem, a castle first built in 1072, overlooking the Mosel (these pages). Facing page bottom: Koblenz, where the Mosel joins the Rhein. On the tongue of land between the two rivers the Monument to German Unity stands floodlit. Above and above right: Traben-Trarbach, and (right) Pünderich. Below: Burg Eltz, depicted on DM 500 bank notes, towering over the lower Mosel (below right).

BRILLANT

BRILLANT

Above: Löffingen in the Schwartzwald (Black Forest). Above left: the Alte Brücke, also known as Karl-Theodor-Brücke, at Heidelberg on the Neckar. Left: Titisee in the Schwartzwald. Below left: a weir on the Murg at the spa town of Gernsbach. Below: the twin-towered Stadtkirche on Augustaplatz, Baden-Baden. Facing page: the frontier-crossing bridge at Laufenburg, straddling the Rhein to link the German and Swiss banks of the river.

Gasthof Laufen

Below: vineyards near Staufen, a town made famous in 1539 as the place where Goethe located the death of infamous alchemist Dr. Faustus. Right: flags in the Casino Gardens at Baden-Baden. This spa town appeared in Mark Twain's book A Tramp in Europe, *and an incident in the Casino is detailed in Dostoevsky's novel* The Gambler. *Below right: fields near Waldshut, just north of the Swiss border. Bottom right: a road winds through a valley near Titisee in the Schwartzwald.*

Above: the Frauenkirche, begun in 1468 in München (Munich) (these pages), capital of Bavaria. Above left: München celebrating Oktoberfest. Left: the Siegestor (Victory Gate), erected in 1850 on Leopoldstrasse. Below left: the Maximilianeum, standing on the site where Ludwig II had wanted to build an opera house for Richard Wagner. Below: the Neues Rathaus, Marienplatz. Facing page: (top) Schloss Nymphenburg, and (bottom) München's Olympic Park.

Above: the Schöner Brunnen ("beautiful fountain") and Frauenkirche in the Hauptmarkt of Nürnberg, Bavaria (these pages) – once the home of Albrecht Dürer. Above left: Klingenberg, and (left) Kitzingen, both on the Main. Below left: Pottenstein. Below and overleaf: Rothenburg ob der Tauber. Facing page top: the fifteenth-century Mainbrücke (bridge over the Main) at Würzburg, decorated with the statues of twelve saints. Facing page bottom: Miltenberg on the Main.

SEIT 1374 LÖWEN-APOTHEKE

Facing page: Bamberg's Altes Rathaus, built on an island in the Regnitz to reconcile the interests of the borough and the episcopal town, then separated by the river. Above: Nesselwang. Above right: Mittenwald in the Bavarian Alps (these pages) – a violin-producing town since Matthias Klotz returned there in 1684 after his apprenticeship to Amati in Cremona. Right: Schloss Linderhof, built by Ludwig II. Below right: Berchtesgaden, by Mount Watzmann, minutes from the Austrian border. Below: Columan Church, near Füssen.

Left: Kloster Ettal, a Baroque Benedictine abbey near Oberammergau. Below: the picturesque church of Maria Gern, north of Berchtesgaden. Facing page: Ramsau church against the Berchtesgaden Alps. Overleaf: winter-ivory Schloss Neuschwanstein, rising above the Schwansee and Alpsee lakes in the Bavarian mountains. The Schloss was designed by the theatre painter C. Jank, who was responsible for the sets for Richard Wagner's opera Tannhäuser. *The castle's singer's hall is based on the "singer's hall" in that opera and is decorated with scenes from the Parsifal legend. The King's study, bedroom, living quarters and dining room are decorated with scenes from* Tristan *and* Lohengrin. *Throughout his life Ludwig II was a dedicated patron of the arts and of Richard Wagner particularly, despite Wagner's many eccentricities. Between Ludwig's insight, Jank's vision and Wagner's music they produced a building which people the world over are delighted to find does not exist only in the imagination of Walt Disney.*